AN APPLETREE DELUXE EDITION

WILD FLOWERS

IRELAND'S FLORA AND FAUNA

A COMPACT ILLUSTRATED GUIDE SHOWING
WILD FLOWERS FROM ACROSS IRELAND AS AN
AID TO IDENTIFICATION

RUTH ISABEL ROSS

AN APPLETREE DELUXE EDITION

WILD FLOWERS

IRELAND'S FLORA AND FAUNA

A COMPACT ILLUSTRATED GUIDE SHOWING
WILD FLOWERS FROM ACROSS IRELAND AS AN
AID TO IDENTIFICATION

Appletree Press

First published in 2007 by
Appletree Press Ltd
The Old Potato Station
14 Howard Street South
Belfast
BT7 1AP

Tel: +44 (0) 28 90 24 30 74
Fax: +44 (0) 28 90 24 67 56
E-mail: reception@appletree.ie
Web Site: www.appletree.ie

First published in 1987 as *Irish Wild Flowers* by Appletree Press Ltd.

A catalogue record for this book is available from the British Library.

WILD FLOWERS – IRELAND'S FLORA & FAUNA

ISBN: 978 1 84758 052 8

Desk & Marketing Editor: Jean Brown
Editor: Jim Black
Designer: Stuart Wilkinson
Production Manager: Paul McAvoy

9 8 7 6 5 4 3 2 1

AP3490

CONTENTS

INTRODUCTION

There is a new and thriving interest being taken in Irish wild flowers, perhaps because of the fashion for conservation.

This pocket guide will help people of different ages and stages to know more. In it there are descriptions of eighty plants. Some of them are well-known favourites. Others are unusual and especially rewarding. There are plants in Cork and Kerry that have their main home in south-west Europe, Wild London Pride and Greater Butterwort to name two; these have been included. And in the Burren, in Co. Clare, plants like Spring Gentian and Mountain Avens, usually associated with high mountains, grow nearly down to sea level; these are described in the Spring and Early Summer sections.

Irish wild flowers are lavish in certain districts. In the north of Ireland the shores near the Giant's Causeway, the banks of Lough Neagh and Lough Erne are outstanding, and, down the west coast, the slopes of Ben Bulben, the Roundstone district and the Burren. Further south, good hunting grounds are the lake shores of Killarney and the coast near Derrynane. But this leaves out too much; there are many prodigal areas.

To find wild flowers one must be energetic. Somebody once complained to me that 'To see the flowers in the Burren you have to get out of the car!' You do indeed, and walk over the rocky pastures and limestone pavements. Some plants will grow obligingly on road verges. Many more will be on lake shores, sea cliffs and dunes, in marshes, on rock ledges, at the edge of woods, on moors – all well away from roads and even from foot paths. This pocket guide is slim enough to be tucked away conveniently when clambering over rough country.

I have avoided arranging the pocket guide into flower families, as is so often done in wild flower books. They can be hard for the non-botanist to follow: how many people would think of looking up Wood

Anemone in the Buttercup family, for instance? It is simpler to divide plants into seasons of flowering, and this is what I have done. The three sections are for plants flowering in spring, early summer and late summer. This is not a foolproof arrangement. A cold season will make every plant flower late, and plants growing on the north side of a hill will bloom later than plants on the south side. If the plant you look for is not in the section you expect, look in the adjoining one.

Plants are arranged alphabetically within the sections and are given their English, their botanical and where possible their Irish names. They are described in simple, unscientific language. Many of them have points of interest; they may have been used as cures or to ward off evil spirits - old wives' tales mostly, but fascinating. The cures must not be taken seriously; many plant treatments are extremely dangerous.

The story of Irish plant discovery is also fascinating. One can imagine the thrill felt by the keen amateur botanist, the Reverend Richard Heaton, when he found such numbers of gentians growing between Gort and Galway; this was before 1650. And in 1700 Edward Lhuyd, a Welshman of avid curiosity, was well rewarded after an exhausting journey. He was the first to discover in Ireland not only, among other plants, St Dabeoc's Heath (usually at home in south-west Europe), but also the pretty, yellow-flowered Shrubby Cinquefoil, rare in Britain, which he found growing on the banks of Lough Corrib.

There have been, and still are fine botanists in Ireland. The definitive work is Dr David Webb's *An Irish Flora*, 6th Edition. To read about Irish plants in depth and detail, look for *The Botanist in Ireland* by Robert Lloyd Praeger; it was reprinted in 1974. Ireland's flora is described by Dr Charles Nelson in *Irish Gardening and Horticulture* published by Folens. (These three books are currently out of print but can be found in libraries.) There is no popular illustrated Irish Flora, unfortunately, but the excellent *Concise British Flora in Colour* by W. Keble Martin includes Irish plants. Another comprehensive illustrated flower book is *The Wild Flowers of Britain and Northern Europe* by Fitter, Fitter and Blamey.

The world distribution of plants given in these texts is taken mainly from Clapham, Tutin and Warburg's *Flora of the British Isles*.

I am greatly indebted to Dr David Webb for advice about this pocket guide.

The reader should note that the flowers are not all drawn to the same scale.

Glossary

Anther: upper portion of the stamen, containing pollen

Basal rosette: leaves forming a rosette shape at the base of the plant

Calyx: outer floral envelope

Filament: stalk of the anther

Floret: small flowers making part of a flower head

Hybrid: a plant produced by fertilising two species

Ovary: part of plant in which seeds are formed

Perennial: a plant surviving more than two years

Pinnate: a compound leaf with leaflets on two sides

Pistil: female organ of the flower, comprising ovary, style and stigma

Sepal: a leaf of the calyx, immediately below the petals

Species: a class of plants having common characteristics

Stamen: male reproductive organ in the flower

Stigma: part of pistil or style which receives pollen

Style: part of plant between ovary and stigma

FLORAL PARTS

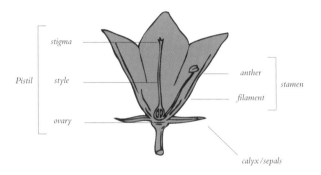

Pistil

stigma

style

ovary

anther

filament

stamen

calyx/sepals

SPRING

Bilberry
Vaccinium myrtillus
Fraochán

Bilberry, or Fraughan, is a small deciduous shrub. The bell-shaped flowers are green, usually tinged with pink. The leaves are oval, slightly toothed and a bright green colour. The fruit is purplish black and edible. It is a twiggy plant, a member of the heath family.

Bilberry grows on acid soil all over the country on heaths, moors and in open woods, and is a far more common plant than *Vaccinium vitis-idaea* (Cowberry) and *Vaccinium oxycoccos* (Cranberry). It is pollinated by bees.

In the past bilberry twigs were cut to make into brooms. The berries are sweet and have traditionally been made into jam. Fraughan picking was an activity in many places every July, sometimes on a regular 'Fraughan Sunday', when children were taken to help gather the fruit.

The flowers come out in April and May.

Bilberry grows on heaths and high ground in Britain, and on the mountains of Europe and northern Asia.

Blackthorn
Prunus spinosa
Draighean

Blackthorn, or Sloe, is a much-branched deciduous shrub often seen growing in hedges. The flowers are a pure white and have five petals. They usually appear before the leaves, which are oval and slightly toothed. There are strong, pointed spines on the branches, and the effect in winter is of black branches and huge black thorns. The bluish-black fruit, sloe, is not poisonous but is bitter.

The shrub grows on waste land as well as in hedges through out the country. It will not grow on peat.

Blackthorn was traditionally made into strong sticks and weapons; sometimes these were buried with corpses. The leaves were considered a cure for indigestion. The fruit was, and still is, made into sloe wine and sloe gin; in the old days it was picked before Hallowe'en, and considered unwholesome afterwards.

The flowers open in March, and look striking on the bare almost leafless branches.

Blackthorn grows over most of Europe and extends to south-west Siberia.

Bogbean
Menyanthes trifoliat
Bearnán lachan

Bogbean, or Buckbean, is an aquatic perennial of the Gentian family. The flowers grow in the form of a spike; they are a pretty pinkish white colour and have white hairs in a fringe. The leaflets grow in threes on a long stalk and the leaves and flowers are held well above the surface of the water.

The plant grows in shallow ponds and lakesides as well as marshes and fens all over Ireland. Country people considered Bogbean a blood purifier, and used it as a remedy for boils.

The flowers open in April and May.

Bogbean grows in Europe, northern and central Asia, Greenland and North America.

Common Wild Violet
Viola riviniana

Common Wild Violet is a low perennial. The petals are violet with a short cream-coloured or whitish spur. The leaves are round to heart-shaped; some of them grow on long stalks in a central non-flowering rosette.

This familiar plant grows on banks and in pastures throughout Ireland as well as on sand dunes and in woods.

The flowers bloom in March and April and again in July and August.

Common Wild Violet is common all over Britain and western Europe, and is found in Morocco and Madeira.

Cowslip
Primula veris

Cowslip is one of Ireland's best-known wild perennials. The bright yellow flowers grow in a cluster and droop. The fresh green leaves are in a rosette; they narrow suddenly at the base to a short stalk.

The plant grows in large drifts in rough pastures where there have been cows in the past, and where the soil is limy. Many pastures have been ploughed up lately and re-seeded and cowslips have become scarcer. However there are still some to be seen. The plant is mainly one of the midlands and is rare in the north and the extreme south. In the past it was traditional to make wine out of cowslip flowers.

Caleb Threlkeld mentioned Cowslip in his *Synopsis Stirpium Hibernicarum*, published in 1726 – "The Cowslips are Friends to the Nerves," he wrote.

The flowers are out in April and May.

Cowslip grows in Britain, except for some counties of Scotland, and in temperate Europe and Asia.

Cuckoo Flower
Cardamine pratensis
Biolar Griaghâin

Cuckoo Flower, sometimes called Lady's Smock, is a medium-sized perennial. The flowers grow loosely together at the top of the stem; they are a pale lilac colour with yellow anthers. The upper leaflets are narrow; the lower ones, coming from the base on long stalks, are rounder.

This elegant spring plant grows in wet meadow and marshes in many places. It is sometimes grown as a garden plant.

The flowers appear in April and May.

Cuckoo Flower grows in similar conditions in Britain. In Europe a related form grows in drier country.

Early Purple Orchid
Orchis mascula

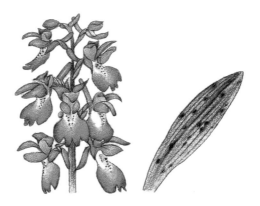

Early Purple Orchid, or Blue Butcher, is a short- to medium-sized perennial, a widespread member of the orchid family. The flowers are a deep purple, or more rarely pinkish mauve or white. The leaves are long and blotched. It is to be seen all over the country near wood and on open pastures, and is especially attractive growing, as it does, in west Clare, where it flowers in late May among the Gentians, wild Geraniums and Mountain Avens; the other plants soften the Orchid's starkness.

The flowers are at their best in April and May.

Early Purple Orchid grows all over Europe, in North Africa and in northern and western Asia.

Heartsease
Viola arvensis

Heartsease, or Field Pansy, is a small delicate annual. The flowers are a cream colour with a yellow and orange tinge. The leaves vary from oval to narrow.

It is an exquisite flower and appears, though infrequently, in ploughed land all over Ireland, but is not a serious weed.

The flowers start blooming in April and can continue until the autumn.

Heartsease is common throughout most of Europe, western Asia, North Africa and Madeira.

Irish Orchid
Neotinea maculata

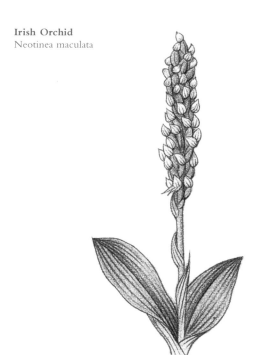

Irish Orchid, or Dense-flowered Orchid, is a short perennial. The flowers are a greenish white or a dull pinkish purple, barely open and crammed together. The leaves of the purple-flowered flowers have purple spots.

The plant grows in rocky or sandy places mainly in the Burren district of Clare, and extends, usually on stony soils, to north Galway and east Mayo. A few outlying colonies have recently been found in Roscommon, Offaly and Cork.

Though not obviously attractive, Irish Orchid is an interesting plant. It does not grow in Britain and is a native mainly of the Mediterranean region. It was not found in Ireland until 1864 when it was discovered by Miss F.M. More at Castle Taylor in Galway. Strangely, this southern plant grows in the same area as the Spring Gentian and Mountain Avens.

Flowering time is May.

Irish Orchid is unknown in Britain but has recently been found in the Isle of Man. It grows in southern Europe, Madeira, the Canaries and North Africa.

Irish Spurge
Euphorbia hyberna
Bainne caoin

Irish Spurge is a medium-sized perennial, often growing in clumps. The flowers are puzzling to the amateur, but the effect is of a yellowish green, leafy group on about five stalks. The stalks join together in a group of five leaves. Below this is a single stem with leaves, large, oblong and slightly downy, growing alternately down it.

The plant grows on lime-free soils in damp places and at the edge of woods. It grows prolifically in Cork and Kerry, and more rarely in south-east Galway and east Donegal.

Irish Spurge is poisonous and, crushed, was and still is used by poachers to kill fish. Country people used to rub it on warts as a cure.

It is in bloom in May.

Irish Spurge is a plant that needs a mild winter, and is rare in Britain. It is found, but only sparsely, in Cornwall, Devon and Somerset. It mainly grows in south-west Europe.

Kingcup
Caltha palustris
Lus buí bealtaine

Kingcup, or Marsh Marigold, is a short- to medium-sized perennial of the buttercup family. The flowers consist of five bright yellow sepals. The leaves grow on long stalks and are thick, scallop-edged and kidney-shaped.

It grows in marshes, fens, lakesides and even in open fields in wet clay soils; it is larger and more luxuriant in the shade. The plant is common all over Ireland. There is a double-flowered variety 'Plena' used for water gardens.

The flowers are open from March until June.

Kingcup grows in Britain, in temperate and Arctic Europe, temperate and Arctic Asia and North America.

Large Bitter Cress
Cardamine amara

Large Bitter Cress is a medium-sized to fairly tall perennial. It resembles Cuckoo Flower in many ways. The flowers of Large Bitter Cress are smaller, however, and grow in a broader cluster; they are nearly always white whereas those of Cuckoo Flower are lilac-coloured. The anthers are different also; instead of being yellow like Cuckoo Flower they are a vivid violet colour. The leaflets are oval and like watercress. The plant grows in wet places, riversides and damp woods, mainly on peat. It is rare in Ireland and only found in the northern counties, chiefly around Lough Neagh.

The flowers bloom from April to June.

Large Bitter Cress grows throughout Europe to Asia Minor, often in damp alder woods.

Lesser Celandine
Ranunculus ficaria

Lesser Celandine, or Pilewort, is a small perennial of the buttercup family. It frequently forms flat, matted clumps. The flowers have eight narrow petals; at first they are bright yellow and later they fade to white. The leaves are dark, thick, heart-shaped and on long stalks.

The plant grows wild all over Ireland on damp shady banks and at the edge of woods. There is a variety which reproduces by little bulbs formed at the base of the leaves.

The flowers appear from March to May.

Lesser Celandine grows throughout Europe and western Asia. It has been introduced into North America.

Primrose
Primula vulgaris

Primrose – the name means 'first rose' – is a small, favourite perennial. The pale yellow flowers are solitary on long fragile stalks. The leaves are bright green, crinkled, and narrowed gradually at the base without a definite stalk.

In most of Europe it is a woodland plant, but the damp air of Ireland lets it grow in pastures and on sand dunes as well as in shady banks. It is especially fine and prolific round Murlough Bay in Antrim.

Flowering time is from March to May.

Primrose grows all over western Europe, the Balkans, the Crimea and North Africa. In eastern Europe, instead of being pale yellow the flowers are often a dull pink.

Seaside Pansy
Viola tricolor subsp
curtisii

Seaside Pansy is a very small perennial, a subspecies of tricolor Pansy. The flowers are bright yellow or violet, or sometimes a combination of the two. The stems and leaves are thin and delicate.

It grows in attractive groups on dunes round the coast of Ireland, and is also occasionally found on lake shores, specifically by Lough Erne, Castlewellan Lake and Lough Neagh.

The flowers open in late April and bloom for several months afterwards.

Seaside Pansy grows round the coast of Britain and on the shores of the Baltic.

Spring Gentian
Gentiana verna

Spring Gentian is a very small perennial. The flowers have five petals and are a vivid blue. The leaves grow mainly in a rosette. The rootstock throws up several flowering stems, making the flowers grow close together.

As Spring Gentian is a mountain plant over much of Europe it is exciting to find it at a low altitude in west Clare, on short turf over limestone. It is the most famous flower of the Burren, and is also found in Galway and parts of Mayo.

The plant was first recorded here in 1650. It had been found growing between Gort and Galway by Richard Heaton, a Yorkshire-born parson and a keen botanist. It is cultivated in gardens in the form 'Angulosa'.

Flowering time is from April to June.

Spring Gentian grows in Britain only in Teesdale, in the north Pennines, where there is grass on limestone, and in central and southern Europe as far as the Caucasus, mainly on the higher mountains.

Thrift
Armeria maritima
Nóinín an chladaigh

Thrift, or Sea Pink, is a small, cushion-like perennial. The round-headed flowers are a bright pink. The leaves grow up from the base and are narrow yet fleshy; there are many of them and with the compact flower heads they form a dense hummock.

The plant grows in great quantities on rocks and cliffs round the coast of Ireland, and occasionally on mountains. The Irish name, when translated, is 'Daisy of the Sea Shore'. It makes a pretty garden plant for border edgings: it is cultivated in the forms 'Alba' (white), 'Merlin' (pink) and 'Vindictive' (a strong red).

The flowers first appear in March and plants are often still flowering in September. Thrift is a common plant round the British coast; it is found on the coast of Europe from Norway to northern Spain.

Wild Cherry
Prunus avium
Crann silín

Wild Cherry, or Gean, is a medium-sized to large deciduous tree. The flowers are white and grow in loose clusters. The leaves are pointed, oval and stalked. The fruit is bitter, and a deep red colour.

The plant is one of Ireland's most handsome and ornamental native trees, with fine spreading branches and a shiny reddish brown bark. It grows, though not prolifically, on good soil in all counties of Ireland except for Longford and north-east Galway.

The flowers bloom in March and April.

Wild Cherry is found in most of Europe, in mountainous North Africa and in western Asia.

Wood Anemone
Anemone nemorosa
Nead cailleach

Wood Anemone is a small fragile perennial. The flowers consist of seven white sepals which close up in the evening; there is an occasional blue form, caerulea. The leaves are deeply cut; they grow on long stalks coming from the main stem in groups of three.

The plant is poisonous. It grows charmingly in drifts at the edge of deciduous woods where the soil is not too acid. It is mainly found in the north of Ireland, and less often in other parts of the country. The naturalist, Robert Lloyd Praeger, mentions a blue form growing in abundance in the Ow river valley above Aughrim, Wicklow. The plant is frequently used for wild gardens, sometimes in the blue form 'Robinsoniana'.

Flowers come out from March to May.

Wood Anemone grows all through the temperate zone of central Europe and western Asia.

Wood Sorrel
Oxalis acetosella
Samhadh coille

Wood Sorrel is a small creeping perennial. The flowers have five white petals with lilac veins. The leaflets, grown in threes, are heart-shaped; they sometimes fold up. Both flowers and leaves have long fragile stalks.

The plant grows in and at the edge of woods throughout Ireland; in the west it can be found on shady banks or among bracken. It is sometimes planted to naturalise in a shady part of the garden but must be treated with caution; it can become a rampant weed.

The flowers are out in April and May.

Wood Sorrel grows throughout western Europe and north and central Asia to Sakhalin and Japan.

EARLY SUMMER

Bitter Vetch
Lathyrus montanus
Carra mhilis

Bitter Vetch is a perennial of the pea family; it is sometimes called Heath Pea. The flowers are a rosy purple; the narrow leaflets grow in pairs. It is remarkable that Bitter Vetch, unlike most other peas and vetches, has no tendrils.

This is a common plant on acid soil, at the edge of woods and in scrubland. It grows in many districts of Ireland, but is not found in Meath or Longford; it is easily found by the lower Lake of Killarney.

The flowers are in bloom from May to July.

Bitter Vetch grows in Britain, except for East Anglia, and in much of western and central Europe.

Bird's-foot Trefoil
Lotus corniculatus
Crúibín cait

Bird's-foot Trefoil, or Bacon and Eggs, is a small, brightly-coloured perennial. Like Bitter Vetch it belongs to the pea family. The flowers are a strong yellow with red streaks and tips. The leaflets grow in fives; as the lower two leaflets slope back the upper ones appear to be in threes, hence the name Trefoil. The pods are long and they join together in the shape of a bird's foot. The plant grows on grass and in rough pastures all over the country; it is widespread and decorative and has many local names.

The flowers bloom between May and September.

Bird's-foot Trefoil is one of the most universal wild flowers. It grows over most of Europe, Asia and parts of Africa, and is found on mountains in the tropics.

Bladder Campion
Silene vulgaris
Cuirean coilleach

Bladder Campion, or White Bottle, is a fragile-looking medium perennial; it is shiny and greyish green. The flowers are usually a pure white, occasionally pink, with five deeply cleft petals. Sepals join to form an inflated calyx, which resembles a bladder; this is purple or yellowish.

Bees are attracted to the plant, which grows in many parts of Ireland beside hedges and roadside verges, usually on lime.

The flowers open in May and can continue until August and September.

Bladder Campion grows in Britain, though not often in the north of the country, and in Europe, Asia and North America.

Bloody Cranesbill
Geranium sanguineum

Bloody Cranesbill is a small, spreading perennial. The flowers are large and of a brilliant crimson purple, very occasionally pink or white; the petals are slightly notched. The leaves are deeply cut.

This is one of the most beautiful of wild Geraniums and looks especially dazzling in late May when it flowers among Gentians and Mountain Avens. A good place to see this is the Burren in west Clare. It grows on limestone in west Clare, the Aran Islands, by Lough Corrib and in Donegal, also in County Dublin on cliffs at Howth and Killiney.

Flowering time is from May to August.

Bloody Cranesbill grows, but rather rarely, over most of Britain except for the south-east. It is found in Europe from Scandinavia east to the Urals and the Caucasus.

Bugle
Ajuga reptans

Bugle is a small perennial. The flowers are a dark blue, and occasionally white or pink; they grow in a spike. The leaves are shiny, oval and a strong green; in some plants they are bronze coloured. Rooting runners are sent out in all directions.

Bugle is found in damp shady meadows and the edge of woods and is common over Ireland in such places. It is cultivated in gardens in various forms. The related and rare Pyramidal or Limestone Bugle (*Ajuga pyramidalis*) has paler blue flowers, and is only found in rocky ground in west Clare and around Galway Bay.

Bugle has flowers from May to July.

The plant grows throughout Britain and much of Europe, south-west Asia, Algeria and Tunisia.

Burnet Rose
Rosa pimpinellifolia
Rós

Burnet Rose, or Scotch Rose, is a small deciduous shrub; if forms so many suckers that it becomes a bushy patch. The flowers are a cream colour, and occasionally pink. The leaflets are small with roundish toothed edges. The stems are immensely prickly. The fruit is unmistakeable, large and black.

Burnet Rose likes to grow on sand dunes and between rocks and limestone pavements. In Ireland it is mainly a seaside plant and it is found round the coast. Occasionally it hybridizes with Dog Rose. The Scotch roses of gardens are derived from Burnet Rose.

It is in flower from May to July.

Burnet Rose grows over most of Britain, but is rare in the south-east. It is widespread in Europe and temperate Asia as far as Manchuria and north-west China.

Charlock
Sinapis arvensis
Praeseach bhuidhe

Charlock, or Wild Mustard, is a tall annual. The flowers are a bright yellow. The leaves are hairy and coarsely toothed; the lower ones are stalked and large, the upper unstalked and narrow.

Charlock is a tiresome weed of cultivated land and used to be rampant where no selective weedkillers are used, but is now less common. It is supposed to have been used as a food in Famine times.

The flowers bloom in May, June and July.

Charlock grows throughout Europe, south-west Asia and Siberia. It has been introduced in North and South America, South Africa, Australia and New Zealand.

Common Butterwort
Pinguicula vulgaris
Liath uisce

Common Butterwort is a small graceful perennial. The flowers are violet coloured with a white throat. The leaves are distinctive. They are a pale yellow-green and form a basal rosette; they are covered with glandular hairs, and these secrete fluid while the leaves roll up at the edges so as to trap and digest insects. The whole plant is a little sticky.

The plant grows in bogs and wet places and is found mainly in the north and west of Ireland. It is less common in the rest of the country and is not found in Cork.

This is one of Ireland's few insectivorous plants. Country people believe, or did believe, that Common Butterwort caused a fatal disease in sheep, possibly dropsy.

The flowers appear in May and June.

Common Butterwort grows in the north and midlands of Britain and in mountainous districts of southern Europe. It is also found in northern Asia and North America as far as British Columbia.

Dog Rose
Rosa canina
Fir dhris

Dog Rose is a tall deciduous shrub with long arching stems. The flowers are larger than those of most other wild roses; they are pink and white and have yellow stamens. The leaflets are small and toothed. Strong, hooked thorns grow out of the branches. The fruit are red egg-shaped hips.

The flowers are exquisite and decorate hedges through out Ireland at midsummer. The hips have occasionally been used to make jam and for medicine; they are a source of vitamin C. They must not be confused with the red berries of Hawthorn, which are indigestible.

The flowers are in bloom in June and July.

Dog Rose is common in Britain except for Scotland. It is widespread in Europe North Africa, south-west Asia and Madeira.

Elder
Sambucus nigra
Trom

Elder is a deciduous shrub or small tree. The flowers are a creamy white and grow in a flattened cluster; they have pale yellow anthers. The leaflets are oval, pointed and toothed. The clustered berries are black and shiny. Stems often shoot up vigorously from the base of the tree.

The plant is widespread in Ireland, growing in hedgerows and waste places where ground has been disturbed. It is often found near houses and rabbit warrens.

It was a custom in rural Ireland to scoop up clay from under an elder bush to soothe an aching tooth. Both the flowers and the fruit have been used in Ireland and many other countries to make drinks; the flowers make a refreshing summer soft drink and the fruit a traditional wine. The fruit must not be muddled up with the very similar berries of the much smaller Danewort (*Sambucus ebulus)*, which are poisonous.

The flowers are in bloom in June and July.

Elder is common in Britain and in most of Europe. It is found in western Asia, West Africa and the Azores.

Field Scabious
Knautia arvensis

Field Scabious, also called Gypsy Rose or Pincushion Flower, is a medium to tall perennial of the Teazel family. The flowers are on long stalks and are a bluish mauve; they form flat cushiony heads. The leaves are variable and deeply lobed. The stalks are a little hairy.

The plant grows over the east, centre and south of the country, nearly always on limestone, on dry grass, road verges and dry banks. It is less common in the north and west. It is visited by butterflies and bees.

The Scabious of gardens, used for herbaceous borders, are derived not from this species but from, mainly, *Scabiosa caucasica* or *columbaria* or *atropurpurea*. The name Scabious comes from a Latin word meaning itch; the English herbalist Culpeper recommended the use of this plant to cure skin disorders.

Flowering starts in June and continues until September.

Field Scabious grows over Britain and northern Europe, the Caucasus and western Siberia.

Greater Butterwort
Pinguicula grandiflora

Greater Butterwort, or Bog Violet, is a larger plant than Common Butterwort; even so it is a small perennial. The flower makes many botanists consider it to be the most beautiful of the Irish flora; it is a rich violet colour.

Like Common Butterwort this plant is insectivorous, the sticky, yellowish leaves rolling inwards to trap and digest insects. Similarly it grows in bogs, damp clearings in woods, wet heaths and rocks. Unlike Common Butterwort it only grows in a limited area: Cork and Kerry, where it is prolific, and Limerick and Clare, where it is rare. It can be cultivated in an Alpine house or as a garden plant in acid, boggy soil.

As well as being beautiful, Greater Butterwort has an interesting history. James Drummond, a Scot and the curator of Cork's botanic garden, was the first to discover it in Ireland; he found it in wet country in County Cork in 1809.

The flowers appear in May and June.

Greater Butterwort is considered a plant mainly of south-western Europe and, except for an introduction in Cornwall, does not grow in Britain. It grows on the Jura, the French Alps, the Pyrenees and the mountains of northern Spain.

Hawthorn
Crataegus monogyna
Sceach gheal

Hawthorn, or Whitethorn, or May-tree, is a deciduous bush or small tree, familiar to most of us. The flowers grow in loose clusters and have pink or purple anthers. The leaves are small and deeply cut. Branches have sharp thorns at intervals. The red berries are indigestible and there is a tradition in Ireland that they cause jaundice.

The plant grows on scrub on most soils except for peat, and is also commonly used for hedges, especially in the countryside.

There are uneasy feelings associated with Hawthorn. In Ireland and England it was considered disastrously unlucky to bring the flowers into a house. Many people are terrified of digging up or cutting down a solitary thorn tree, perhaps because thorns are linked with sacred places, graves, hidden treasure, trysting places. Some say that the crown of thorns was a hawthorn. In any case the flowering thorn tree symbolised the end of winter to many primitive peoples; this may have given it a sacred value from pagan times onward in several countries.

The flowers bloom in May and June.

Hawthorn is common in Britain, except for northern Scotland, and grows through Europe eastwards to Afghanistan.

Hoary Rockrose
Helianthemum canum

Hoary Rockrose is a very small shrub. The flowers have five petals and are a pale yellow. The small narrow leaves are greenish grey above and white beneath. The stems creep and make the plant form a small mat.

This pretty little plant makes tiny spreading clumps in the bare limestone pavements of west Clare, where it is prolific. It is found also on Inishmore.

Hoary Rockrose was first reported in Ireland in 1806 by the enthusiastic plant hunter James Mackay, Curator of Dublin's Trinity College Botanic Garden. The plant should not be confused with the larger-flowered Common Rockrose, *Helianthemum chamaecistus*, common in Britain but in Ireland only found in one place near Ballintra, in Donegal. The name Helianthemum is derived from the Greek word for sunflower.

The flowers are in bloom in May and June.

Hoary Rockrose is rare in Britain. It grows on limestone pastures in Wales, Yorkshire and parts of Cumbria. It is found, given the right conditions, in Europe, including Sicily and Macedonia, in the Caucasus, and in Morocco and Algeria.

Kerry Lily
Simethis
planifolia

Kerry Lily is a small perennial. The flowers grow in a loose cluster and have six petals, white with purple veins. The leaves are narrow, greyish and grass-like; they grow up from the base and curl slightly.

This is one of the rare plants of the British Isles, and in Ireland only grows in a small area of rocky ground near Derrynane, County Kerry.

Kerry Lily is mainly a southern European plant and was not discovered in Ireland until the mid 19th century. In 1848 the *London Journal of Botany* reports it as growing wild near Derrynane in ground which has "never been turned up". The discoverer was the Reverend Thaddeus O'Mahony, Professor of Irish at Trinity College, Dublin, and a keen naturalist.

The flowers appear in June and July.

Kerry Lily only grows in one place in Britain, where it was almost certainly introduced. It is found in western and southern France and many Mediterranean countries including Morocco, Algeria and Tunisia.

Kidney Saxifrage
Saxifraga hirsuta

Kidney Saxifrage is a small perennial related to London Pride. The loosely clustered flowers are white or a very pale pink. The leaves are hairy and a handsome kidney shape; they are scalloped, bright green and grow on long stalks.

The plant is not widespread and is found in rocky, damp shade and by mountain streams, always in Cork and Kerry. The Killarney woods are good hunting grounds.

The flowers bloom from May to July.

Kidney Saxifrage is not found in Britain but is native in the Pyrenees and northern Spain.

Kidney Vetch
Anthyllis vulneraria

Kidney Vetch, or Lady's Fingers, is a medium-sized perennial. The flowers are usually yellow but near the sea they are sometimes white, crimson or purple; the flowerheads often grow in pairs. The leaves are narrow and pinnate. The whole plant is slightly downy.

Kidney Vetch grows near rocks and on dry pastures, especially near the coast. The name *vulneraria* was given to show that wounds were sometimes treated with this plant.

Flowering time is from June to August.

Kidney Vetch grows on sandy soils and near the sea in Britain. It spreads through Europe to the Caucasus and grows in North Africa.

London Pride
Saxifraga spathularis
Cabáiste mhadra rua

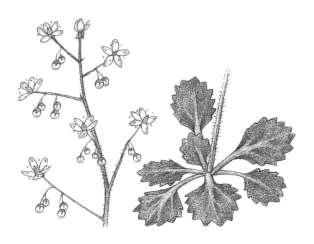

London Pride, or Wild London Pride, also called St Patrick's Cabbage and Fox's Cabbage, is a small- to medium-sized perennial. It is more widespread than Kidney Saxifrage. The flowers are held up in a loose cluster above graceful stalks; they are pink and white with crimson spots. The leaves grow in a basal rosette; they narrow towards the base. The stems are reddish and the plant gives a reddish impression.

This is one of Ireland's most elegant native plants, and is confusingly variable. It can easily be found among mainly acid rocks in Cork and Kerry, and less prolifically northward to Donegal, also in the Galtees, Waterford and Wicklow. The plant grows luxuriantly in the shade, especially in the woods round Killarney. The London Pride of gardens is a hybrid between this plant and *Saxifraga umbrosa* which grows only in the Pyrenees.

In 1696 the Dublin physician Thomas Molyneux recorded this saxifrage; he had found it growing over a mountain in Kerry.

The flowers open from May to July.

Wild London Pride is not native to Britain. It grows in northern Spain and in the mountains of northern Portugal.

Marsh Pea
Lathyrus palustris

Marsh Pea is a tall climbing perennial. The flowers are a lilac blue. The leaflets are narrow and grow in pairs; the leaves end in branched tendrils.

The plant is rare and grows in boggy meadows and fens. It was once growing freely round Lough Neagh, but may not be found there now. Look for it around Lough Erne and the Westmeath lakes.

The flowers appear in June.

Marsh Pea is a northern plant. It occurs in the east of England, in Europe to northern Norway, Arctic Russia and Siberia, and east to Japan. It is also found in eastern North America.

Milkwort
Polygala vulgaris
Glúineach

Milkwort, or Common Milkwort, is a small perennial. The flowers are blue, or mauve, or even white with blue tips; they grow up in a spike. The leaves are narrow.

Common Milkwort is widely found on dry grass and sandhills on calcareous soils all over the country. The name of the plant *Polygala* is from the Greek and means "much milk"; it was believed to be good for the milk yield. In Ireland the juice of Milkwort was one of those used to cure warts. Common Milkwort can easily be confused with Heath Milkwort (*Polygala serpyllifolia*), a plant with shorter spikes and darker flowers, which grows in acid soil.

The flowers are in bloom from May to August.

Common Milkwort grows widely in Europe, west Asia and North Africa.

Mountain Avens
Dryas octopetala
Leaithín

Mountain Avens is a spreading undershrub. The flowers are pure white and have about eight petals. The leaves are shaped like oak leaves and are dark green above and white beneath. The fruit is long and feathery.

The plant is rare and only grows in rocky places, usually on high ground; in west Clare, however, its main home in Ireland, it comes down almost to sea level. It is occasionally found on limestone through Galway, Leitrim and Sligo, and very sparsely, on Slieve League in Donegal and Binevenagh in Antrim.

Mountain Avens is beautiful enough to be a sought-after rock plant for gardens. The name Dryas was given it because of the striking, oak-like leaves; a Dryad was the nymph of oak woods in the ancient world. Like Spring Gentian, it was found by the Reverend Richard Heaton shortly before 1650; he compared the feathery fruit to that of the Wild Clematis.

The flowers are in bloom in May and June.

Mountain Avens is rare in Britain, locally found on high ground in northern Wales and Teesdale; it grows down to sea level in northern Scotland. It grows in Arctic Europe, and on the higher mountains further south.

Ox-eye Daisy
Leucanthemum vulgare
Nóinín mór

Ox-eye Daisy has many names – Moon Daisy, Dog Daisy and Marguerite. In Scotland, where the daisy is called Gowan, Ox-eye Daisy is known as Horse-gowan.

The Ox-eye Daisy is a medium-sized perennial. The flowers consist of a bright yellow disc of florets surrounded by many white rays. The leaves are sparse and toothed. The stems, like the leaves, are slightly downy. It is rampant on verges and on fertile pastures all over the country.

Flowers start blooming in May and continue for the rest of the summer.

Ox-eye Daisy is native to Britain. It has been introduced in North America and New Zealand.

Ragged Robin
Lychnis floscuculi

Ragged Robin is a medium to tall perennial. The red flower petals are deeply cleft, giving a ragged look. The upper leaves are sparse and narrow, the lower ones rounder. The stem, reddish looking and slightly downy, is sticky towards the top. The calyx is red and bloated with purple veins.

The plant grows in many marshes and fens and is conspicuous. Butterflies visit the flowers which produce honey.

The flowers appear in June and July.

Ragged Robin is common in Europe, and has been introduced in North America.

Rose Campion
Silene dioica
Coireán coilleach

Rose Campion, or Red Campion, is a tall perennial. The flowers are bright pink and form loose clusters; the petals are cleft. The oval leaves are downy; they grow stalkless, opposite each other on the stems which are also downy. The calyxes are swollen and reddish.

This colourful plant grows in good soil in wood clearings, hedge banks and sea cliffs. It is widespread in the north-east of Ireland but much more uncommon in the rest of the country.

The flowers appear in May; bloom continues until October.

Rose Campion grows in Britain, Europe, North Africa and western Asia.

Scarlet Pimpernel
Anagallis arvensis
Rinn-rúisc

Scarlet Pimpernel, also called Shepherd's Weatherglass and Poor Man's Weatherglass, is a small annual. The scarlet flowers have five petals. The leaves are oval, have no stalks and grow opposite each other. There is a prostrate stem which throws up flowering shoots.

The plant grows in dry conditions in disturbed ground, sand dunes and ploughed fields, and is very common in the south of Ireland, less so in the north. The name Weatherglass is aptly given to this pretty flower, as the petals close when the sun goes in; they close regularly in mid-afternoon also.

Flowering starts in May and continues until the autumn.

Scarlet Pimpernel grows in most non-tropical countries.

Sea Campion
Silene vulgaris subsp
maritima

Sea Campion is a subspecies of Bladder Campion and is a smaller perennial. The flowers of Sea Campion are often solitary whereas those of Bladder Campion form a loose cluster. The petals differ also – those of Sea Campion are broader. Sea Campion's leaves are narrower; many of them are non-flowering and these form a kind of mat. The swollen calyxes of Sea Campion have broader mouths.

Sea Campion is a plant of the seaside and of rocky coasts. It grows all round the coasts of Ireland and is one of the many beautiful plants flourishing near the Glens of Antrim. It is grown in gardens in the double white form 'Flore pleno'.

The flowers appear from June to August. Sea Campion grows round the coast of Britain and round Europe's Atlantic coast.

Sea Rocket
Cakile maritima

Sea Rocket is a slightly bushy, medium-sized annual. The flowers are lilac to white and have four petals; they form a relaxed cluster of four to six blooms. The leaves are unmistakably shiny, fleshy, and deeply lobed. The stem is prostrate, with a tap root that goes down a long way for water, for this is a plant that grows on sand and shingle above the drift line.

Sea Rocket is found round the Irish coast, more commonly in the north and east. The name Cakile is said to derive from an Arabic word for the plant, or one similar.

Flowers bloom from June to August.

Sea Rocket grows round the Atlantic coasts of Europe.

Shrubby Cinquefoil
Potentilla fruticosa

Shrubby Cinquefoil is a small deciduous shrub, and one rare in the British Isles. The five-petalled flowers are yellow and grow in loose clusters. The leaflets, greyish and slightly downy, usually grow in fives. The bark peels every third year or so.

The shrub is grown in gardens, as are many hybrids with related species. In the wild it is best known as growing in cold countries and at high altitudes. In Ireland it only thrives on stony or rocky ground likely to flood, as the roots need to be damp. It is still found by turloughs and lakes in north Clare and on the eastern shore of Lough Corrib.

Shrubby Cinquefoil was first discovered in Ireland in 1700 by Edward Lhuyd, Assistant Keeper of the Ashmolean Museum, Oxford, who was on a plant-hunting expedition in the west of the country. He recorded it as growing on the shores of Lough Corrib between limestone rocks.

The flowers of this decorative plant bloom from early June until August.

In Britain, Shrubby Cinquefoil grows on Helvellyn, in Upper Teesdale and, rarely, in the Lake District. It is a native of the Baltic countries, Greenland, Labrador and Alaska, and of many mountain ranges in the northern hemisphere.

Wall Pepper
Sedum acre

Wall Pepper, or Biting Stonecrop, is a small evergreen perennial. The flowers are star-like with five petals and are a bright yellow. The leaves are small, thick, fleshy and have a peppery taste. The creeping stems make the plant form an attractive, yellow-flowered mat.

Wall Pepper grows on mortared walls, poor soil, shingle, railway embankments and limestone generally and is very common in Ireland. There is a garden form 'Aureum'.

Roger Phillips in his book *Wild Flowers of Britain* claims that in Suffolk and Dorset this plant used to be known as 'Welcome home husband, though never so drunk.'

The flowers appear in June and July. Wall Pepper grows all over Europe, western Asia and North Africa. It is naturalised in North America.

Water Avens
Geum rivale
Machall uisce

Water Avens, or Billy's Button, is a small- to medium-sized perennial. The flowers are nodding and grow on long stalks, they are bell-shaped and a soft red colour. The few leaves are lobed and toothed. The plant is downy.

This delicate-coloured and unusual plant grows, though not prolifically, in damp places near woods and streams in many parts of Ireland; it is more widespread in the north of the country than the south. It is related to Wood Avens. A few varieties of Water Avens are grown in gardens.

Flowering time is May and June.

Water Avens is widespread in Britain, though not in the south-east, and in most of Europe and much of North America.

Welsh Poppy
Meconopsis cambrica

Welsh Poppy is a medium-sized perennial. The flowers are large and an attractive mid-yellow colour. The leaves are deeply divided. The whole plant is slightly downy.

Welsh Poppy grows in wet rocky places and shady banks, and is uncommon except as a garden escape. There are cultivated double forms of this lovely plant in yellow and orange.

The flowers bloom in June and July.

Welsh Poppy is native to Wales and to the west of England, also to western France, Portugal and northern Spain.

Wild Thyme
Thymus praecox or
Thymus drucei

Wild Thyme is a very small undershrub. The flowers are a purplish rose colour. The tiny leaves are hard and sometimes hairy. The plant forms an aromatic tuft or mat.

The plant grows in sunny dry places, usually, but not always, near the coast; it is not found in Tyrone or Carlow. There are cultivated varieties for the garden: 'Albus' with white flowers, the shell-pink 'Connie Hall', the crimson 'Coccineus' and others.

Flowering time is from June to August.

It is native to western Europe from Norway to north-west Spain.

Yellow Flag
Iris pseudacorus
Seilistrom

Yellow Flag is a tall handsome perennial. The flowers are a strong yellow colour. The leaves are stiff and sword-like. It grows by fresh water, river and lakesides, marshes and ditches; sometimes it takes over large parts of wet fields. This can be a wonderful sight in June.

In the old days leaves of this plant were sometimes used for thatching and bedding. Country people traditionally placed flowers of Yellow Flag outside their houses as a decoration for the Corpus Christi festival. Caleb Threlkeld called the plant Yellow Water Flower de Luce. There are cultivated varieties of this Iris, 'Bastardii', with pale yellow flowers, a deeper yellow 'Golden Queen' and 'Variegata' with yellow striped foliage.

The flowers are in bloom from June to August. Yellow Flag grows in the same conditions in Britain and in Europe, North Africa and western Asia.

Yellow Pimpernel
Lysimachia nemorum

Yellow Pimpernel (another name is Woodland Loosestrife) is a small creeping perennial. The flowers are five-petalled, wide open and a clear yellow. The leaves are oval and grow opposite each other. It must not be confused with the related Creeping Jenny (*Lysimachia nummularia*) which has cup-shaped and larger flowers.

Yellow pimpernel is common in Ireland on damp mountain pastures and in woods with damp soils.

Flowering time is from May to September.

It is native to the damper parts of Britain and is found throughout Europe.

LATE SUMMER

Chamomile
Chamaemelum nobile
Común meall milis

Chamomile is a creeping, small- to medium-sized perennial. The white-petalled daisy-type flowers are on longish stalks. The aromatic leaves grow alternately on the stem and are finely fragmented. The plant is downy.

This plant grows on gravelly pastures, roadsides and heaths, and is often seen in the south and west of Ireland, more rarely in the rest of the country. The cultivated non-flowering variety 'Treneague' is sometimes planted in gardens to make scented chamomile lawns.

Chamomile tea, made out of the dried flower heads, is still used as a cure for indigestion in many countries. In Ireland it was considered a remedy for pleurisy, whooping cough and consumption, and was given as a tonic; even inhaling the aroma was said to be health-giving.

The flowers bloom from June to August.

Chamomile is native to western Europe from the Netherlands southwards, to North Africa and to the Azores.

Common Mallow
Malva sylvestris
Hocas

Common Mallow, or Rags and Tatters, is a medium-sized perennial. The flowers have five heart-shaped petals; they are a purple colour with darker veins. The kidney-shaped leaves are large, toothed, lobed and have long stalks. The plant is slightly hairy.

This good-looking plant grows on roadsides and waste places, often near houses or ruins. It is fairly common in coastal regions of the south, less common inland and rare in the north.

Flowering time is from June to October.

Common Mallow grows in Britain and throughout Europe.

Foxglove
Digitalis purpurea
Méaracán dearg

Foxglove is a tall biennial, occasionally a perennial. The flowers grow in
a spike and are a pinkish purple, or occasionally white; they are tubular,
and spotted inside. The leaves are oval, soft and downy.

This rich-looking plant grows, and looks magnificent, on shady banks
and at the edge of woods where the soil is acid. It is an effective garden
plant for the shade and is cultivated in many forms. The name *Digitalis*
comes from the Latin for thimble, from the shape of the flowers. The
plant is poisonous. The drug Digitalin is made from the leaves and
used to treat heart disease. In Ireland Foxglove was sometimes used as
a remedy for weak hearts; this must have killed many.

The flowers are out in late June, July and August.

Grass of Parnassus
Parnassia palustris

Grass of Parnassus is a small perennial. The flowers grow singly on long stalks; they have five white petals with darker veins. The leaves are smooth-edged and heart-shaped.

The plant grows in damp pastures, sometimes high up on mountains, and equally often lower down by river or lakesides. It is found in the west and centre of Ireland, but is not native to parts of the south-west and north-east.

This exquisite plant may have been referred to in the 1st century AD by Dioscorides. He wrote, "The grass which grows on Parnassus … bears leaves like to Ivy, a white flower and of a sweet scent." (John Goodyear's translation.)

The flowers bloom in July and August. Grass of Parnassus grows in some districts of Britain, in Europe and in temperate parts of Asia.

Greater Spearwort
Ranunculus lingua

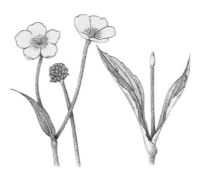

Greater Spearwort is a tall perennial of the Buttercup family. The flowers are yellow, shiny and twice the size of a Field Buttercup. The bluish green leaves, unlike deeply cut buttercup leaves, are long, pointed and toothed, just slightly; they seem to grip the stem. The stem creeps and roots in the mud, and then grows upwards.

This striking plant is found in ditches and fens in the Irish midlands, and has travelled up to Dublin via the canals, but is less seen in the rest of the country. The cultivated variety 'Grandiflora' makes a decorative marginal plant for garden ponds and lakes.

The flowers bloom from June to August.

Greater Spearwort is becoming rare in Britain. It grows throughout Europe and in Siberia.

Harebell
Campanula rotundifolia
Méaracán gorm

Harebell, in Scotland called Bluebell, is a small, well-known perennial. The flowers are pale blue and bell-like. The lower leaves are round and on long stalks, the upper ones narrow. The stems are fragile.

This exquisite plant grows in dry grassy places, sandhills and poor soil generally. It is common near the north and west coasts but not often seen in the rest of the country. The name Campanula comes from the Latin word meaning a bell. There are several cultivated varieties; one, 'Alba', has white flowers.

The flowers come out in July and August.

Harebell grows in Britain and in the temperate regions of Europe.

Herb Bennet

Geum urbanum

Machall coille

Herb Bennet (once called Herb Benedict), or Wood Avens, is a small-to medium-sized perennial. The flowers are small and pale yellow with five wide-open petals; they are solitary on long stalks. The leaves are deeply toothed and lobed. The seedheads are bristly and long-lasting.

Herb Bennet sometimes hybridises with Water Avens. It grows at the edge of woods, in shady damp places and is common all over the country. The roots smell of cloves; in some countries they were hung by the door to repel evil spirits.

The flowers bloom from June to September.

Herb Bennet is found in Britain, in most parts of Europe, in western Asia and in North Africa.

Lax-flowered Sea Lavender
Limonium humile

Lax-flowered Sea Lavender is a small perennial. The flowers are lilac-coloured, close together and grow in flat-topped clusters. The leaves are narrow and stalked. Stems form branches low down with flowers growing on them. In this the plant differs from the similar Common Sea Lavender (*Limonium vulgare*) as flowering branches of the latter form high up on the stem. In any case there is no Common Sea Lavender in Ireland. Lax-flowered Sea Lavender forms attractive clumps on salt marshes and on muddy shores round the east, south and west coasts of Ireland.

Flowering time is July to September.

Lax-flowered Sea Lavender is a northern plant. It grows on the north coast of Britain and on the European coast from Sweden and Norway to Brittany.

Lesser Stitchwort
Stellaria graminea

Lesser Stitchwort is a small perennial. The flowers have five deeply cleft white petals, no longer than the sepals; the anthers are red and the flowers grow in a loose cluster. Seedheads hang down at first, then rise to become horizontal. The leaves are narrow, pointed and stalkless.

This, like the larger Greater Stitchwort (*Stellaria holostea*), is a common plant in Ireland and grows on light grassy soils, usually not on lime. The plant was given the name *Stellaria* because of its star-like flowers.

Flowers appear from June to August.

Lesser Stitchwort grows throughout Britain, Europe and Asia.

Meadow Cranesbill
Geranium pratense

Meadow Cranesbill is a medium-sized perennial. The flowers are large and violet-blue. The leaves are deeply cut, the stems slightly hairy. The fruit droop at first and then become erect. The plant grows on banks and waste places and is one of the loveliest wild Geraniums.

In Ireland it is only native in a small area near the Giant's Causeway in Antrim, where it is prolific. It is seen occasionally elsewhere but is almost certainly a garden escape. It is grown in gardens in many varieties, among them the double blue 'Flore pleno', and the white, dark-veined 'Kashmir White'.

The flowers open from June to September.

Meadow Cranesbill is widespread in Europe and parts of Asia, including the Himalayas and Japan.

Meadow Vetchling
Lathyrus pratensis
Pis bhuidhe

Meadow Vetchling, or Yellow Pea, is a clambering perennial of the Pea family. The bright yellow flowers grow in a loose cluster, or spike. The leaflets are narrow and grow with a branched tendril between them. It is common in damp meadows and ditches all over Ireland.

The plant must not be confused with Bird's-foot Trefoil (*Lotus corniculatus*); the leaflets of Meadow Vetchling are much narrower. It has slight similarities with the Everlasting Pea of gardens.

The flowers bloom from June to September.

Meadow Vetchling is found in much of Northern Europe, Siberia, the Himalayas and Ethiopia.

Pink Butterwort
Pinguicula lusitanica

Pink Butterwort, or Pale Butterwort, is the smallest of the three Irish Butterworts; it is also the last to flower. The flowers are a pale lilac and yellow colour. The leaves are a drab green; they form a basal rosette which stays visible through the winter.

Like its fellows it grows in damp conditions, in bogs and by mountain streams. It is often found in the extreme west but is more rare in the rest of the country. Like the others it is insectivorous, oozing sticky fluids which, with leaf edges that roll inward, trap and digest insects. It is as elegant-looking as its fellow Butterworts.

Flowering time is from late June to September. Pink Butterwort is a western European plant. It grows in some western parts of England and Scotland, in western France, western Spain and Portugal.

Pipewort
Eriocaulon aquaticum

Pipewort is an interesting perennial water plant. The flowers are whitish and button-like; they are held well above the water and are often damp and glistening. The narrow and translucent leaves grow in a totally submerged rosette.

The plant is found in shallow, still water on peaty soil. It is native to the west of Ireland in shallow lakes from Donegal southward to Kerry, but is only really prolific in Connemara. The enthusiastic and meticulous botanist, Dr Walter Wade, Professor of Botany to the Dublin Society, discovered the plant there in 1801; he was delighted to find such numbers of this unusual species which, he claimed, had only been seen before on the Isle of Skye.

The flowers appear in July and August.

Pipewort is unknown on the continent of Europe and in Britain except in a small part of the West Highlands of Scotland. There is an identical, or closely related, plant in North America.

Restharrow
Ononis repens
Sreang bogha

Restharrow (known as Cammock in parts of Britain) is a small shrub of the Pea family, partly creeping and partly erect. The flowers are pink and grow from the leaf axils. The leaflets are oval and slightly toothed. The stem and the young shoots are hairy; sometimes there are soft spines.

Restharrow is meant to indicate poor or neglected land. It grows in dry waste places and on sandhills and is often found in the south-east of the country, more rarely in the south, west and north. It is absent from many midland counties.

The rootstock of Restharrow often creeps under ground, and is so strong that it will "wrest the harrow" from its proper direction. Hence the name of the plant. This is the only type of Restharrow native to Ireland; Spiny Restharrow (*Ononis spinosa*) is not found here.

Flowering time is July to September.

Restharrow grows in Britain and much of Europe, east to Estonia and south to Bulgaria, often on calcareous soils.

Rosebay Willowherb
Epilobium angustifolium

Rosebay Willowherb (sometimes called Fireweed) is very tall perennial. The flowers grow up in a spike, but loosely; there are four purple sepals and four irregular rosy petals. The leaves are pointed and willow-like; they grow alternately up the main stem.

Rosebay has long been a rare and colourful plant found on mountain ledges. Recently it has taken to growing in hedges and on the margin of woods and bogs, but not nearly as wildly as in Britain, where it has spread in the last fifty years through disturbed land, wood clearings and roadsides. The name 'Fireweed' was given it because it thrives on ground where fire has been.

The flowers appear from July to September.

Rosebay is found in Europe, Asia and North America.

St Dabeoc's Heath
Daboecia cantabrica
Fraoch gallda

St Dabeoc's Heath is a small straggly shrub, a form of heather that grows up well through other plants. The drooping flowers are large and rosy purple; they are more spaced out than those of other heathers. The leaves are dark above and white beneath. The stems are straggly and weak.

St Dabeoc's Heath grows among rocks, by the sides of acid lakes and on heaths. It is prolific in Connemara, in some places growing to the edge of the Atlantic, and is found in Mayo, but more rarely. It is cultivated as a garden plant in many varieties, among them the deep purple-flowered 'Atropurpurea' and 'Alba Globosa' with broad white flowers.

This heath was first discovered in Ireland by Edward Lhuyd on his journey round Ireland in 1700. He learnt that women wore the plant to protect their chastity.

Flowering time is from June to October.

St Dabeoc's Heath is not native to Britain. It grows in western France, north-west and central Spain and north-west Portugal.

Sea Holly
Eryngium maritimum
Cuileann trá

Sea Holly, once called Sea Eryngo or Sea Holm, is a small to medium-sized perennial. The flowers have pale blue dense heads surrounded by spiky, mauve bracts. The shiny bluish leaves grow in threes up the stems, and have stiff spines. The stems are stiff also and, because they come from a creeping rootstock, many of them quickly form a little bush.

The plant grows on sand, and is found in many places round the coast. This is the only Eryngium to be found in Ireland. The Field Eryngo or Watling Street Thistle (*Eryngium campestre*) is very scarce in Britain and unknown in Ireland. Sea Holly is cultivated by gardeners as a border plant with strong effects, as are related Eryngiums of African and Asian origin.

The flowers are in bloom in July and August.

Sea Holly grows on sand all round the coasts of Europe.

Self-heal
Prunella vulgaris
Ceannbhán beag

Self-heal is a small creeping perennial. The flowers are violet-coloured and occasionally pink or white. The leaves are oval, pointed and slightly toothed; the lower ones are stalked. The stems are hairy. The plant grows on damp pastures, roadsides and heaths and is abundant in these places.

Self-heal, as its name implies, was once considered to have important medicinal qualities. In Ireland it was used as a remedy for sudden strokes. In other countries the plant was used for dressing wounds. The name Prunella is said to come from the German *Bräune*, a word for quinsy or croup, which the plant was reputed to cure. Other names for Self-heal were Hook-heal and Sicklewort. Culpeper wrote that doctors were unnecessary if one had Self-heal. This view is now discredited.

The flowers bloom from late June to September, occasionally until October.

Self-heal grows throughout Britain, southern Europe, temperate Asia, North Africa, North America and Australia.

Tormentil
Potentilla erecta
Néalfhartach

Tormentil is a perennial, sometimes erect, sometimes forming a mat. The flowers have four bright yellow petals and four sepals. The leaflets grow in groups of three or five; they are unstalked and deeply cut.

The plant grows in acid or slightly acid soil on many banks, heaths and hills and likes drier root conditions than other Potentillas. It differs from others also in having four petals instead of five. Tormentil has tannin in the roots; in the past country people in Ireland used it to treat burns.

The flowers are in bloom from June to September.

Tormentil grows throughout Britain, Europe, north-west Asia and North Africa.

Traveller's Joy
Clematis vitalba

Traveller's Joy (sometimes called Old Man's Beard or Virgin's Bower) is a strongly climbing perennial. The flowers consist of four greenish white sepals, usually bending back; the stamens are prominent. The leaflets are grouped in fives, the groups growing opposite each other. The fruit are like balls of down all through the autumn and winter, and give the plant its name Old Man's Beard.

The plant grows by its twisting leafstalks to dramatic heights, sometimes up trees and telegraph poles, making vast festoons. It is a scrub, hedge and woodland plant and likes growing on limestone. It is not native to Ireland, always a garden escape, and is scattered in the south and north of Ireland but absent from Donegal, Galway and some midland counties.

The flowers appear in July and August.

Traveller's Joy grows in the south of England, in Europe from the Netherlands southwards and in North Africa.

Water Germander
Teucrium scordium

Water Germander is a sprawling perennial. The flowers are a pale purple and grow in whorls up leafy stems. The leaves are oval, stalkless and slightly toothed. The stems and leaves are soft and hairy.

The plant grows by fresh water at lakesides. It is very rare, but can be found along the banks of the River Shannon, mainly beside Lough Ree and Lough Derg, and in turloughs in Clare and Tipperary. It is pollinated by bees.

Flowering time is in July and August.

Water Germander is rare in Britain. It is more widespread in Europe south of Scandinavia.

Water Lobelia
Lobelia dortmanna

Water Lobelia is an aquatic perennial of the Campanula family. The flowers are a pale mauve and hang elegantly on a slender stalk, well above water level. The leaves are in a completely submerged basal rosette.

The plant roots in acid shallow water. It is frequently found in turf-margined lakes from Kerry northwards, through Clare, Galway and Mayo to Donegal, and is common in most of Achill Island's lower-level lakes. It is rare in the rest of the country. Lobelias are named after Mathias de l'Obel, the distinguished Flemish botanist who studied in the 16th century.

The flowers appear in July and August.

Water Lobelia is found in lakes in north-west Britain and in north-west Europe.

Water Mint
Mentha aquatica
Mismín dearg

Water Mint is a short- to medium-sized perennial. The flowers are dense and lilac-coloured; they grow at intervals high up on the stem finishing with a group of flowers at the top. The stamens protrude; the calyx is long and hairy. The leaves are stalked, toothed and grow opposite each other. The stems are stiff.

Like many mints, Water Mint likes wet ground, so that it is found in marshes and lake shores throughout Ireland. The leaves give off a strong minty scent when crushed. Water Mint sometimes hybridises with the ordinary garden mint, Spear Mint (*Mentha spicata*) to give peppermint, as well as with Corn Mint (*Mentha arvensis*).

The flowers appear in July, August and September. Water Mint grows in Europe, south-west Asia, North and South Africa and Madeira.

Wood Sage
Teucrium scorodonia
Úr sléibhe

Wood Sage, or Germander, is a small to medium perennial. The paired flowers are a greenish yellow and grow on branched spikes. The anthers are maroon-coloured and prominent. The leaves are heart-shaped, toothed, wrinkled and downy. The stem is reddish and square.

The plant usually grows in acid soil and is found on dry heathy places and open woods. It is fairly common in the mountains but scarcer in the lowlands and hard to find in the centre of the country.

Flowering time is July and August.

Wood Sage is widespread in western Europe and in Croatia.

INDEX